T0198899

Ruby's Recital

Ruby Tilghman

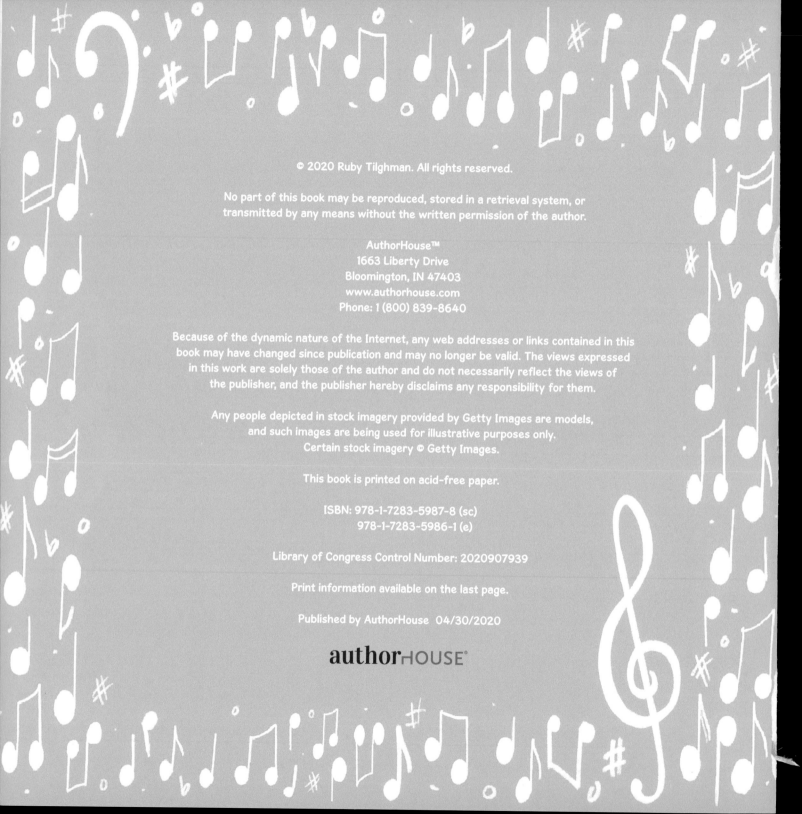

AuthorHouse™
1663 Liberty Drive
Bloomington, IN 47403
www.authorhouse.com
Phone: 1 (800) 839-8640

Because of the dynamic nature of the Internet, any web addresses or links contained in this
book may have changed since publication and may no longer be valid. The views expressed
in this work are solely those of the author and do not necessarily reflect the views of
the publisher, and the publisher hereby disclaims any responsibility for them.

Any people depicted in stock imagery provided by Getty Images are models,
and such images are being used for illustrative purposes only.
Certain stock imagery © Getty Images.

This book is printed on acid-free paper.

ISBN: 978-1-7283-5987-8 (sc)
978-1-7283-5986-1 (e)

Library of Congress Control Number: 2020907939

Print information available on the last page.

Published by AuthorHouse 04/30/2020

authorHOUSE®

The big recital was coming up at Ruby's school. She couldn't wait to sign up. Her one problem was she didn't know which instrument she would play.

All of Ruby's classmates had already decided what instrument they would play, but she still didn't know. She decided she would try all of the instruments until she found one that was exactly what she was looking for.

So she tried the drums. They looked so cool and kept a steady beat. It seemed like the drums were exactly what she was looking for.

But the BOOM, BOOM, BOOM of the drums
was just too loud.

So she tried the piccolo. It was small and delicate and made a beautiful sound. It seemed like the piccolo was exactly what she was looking for.

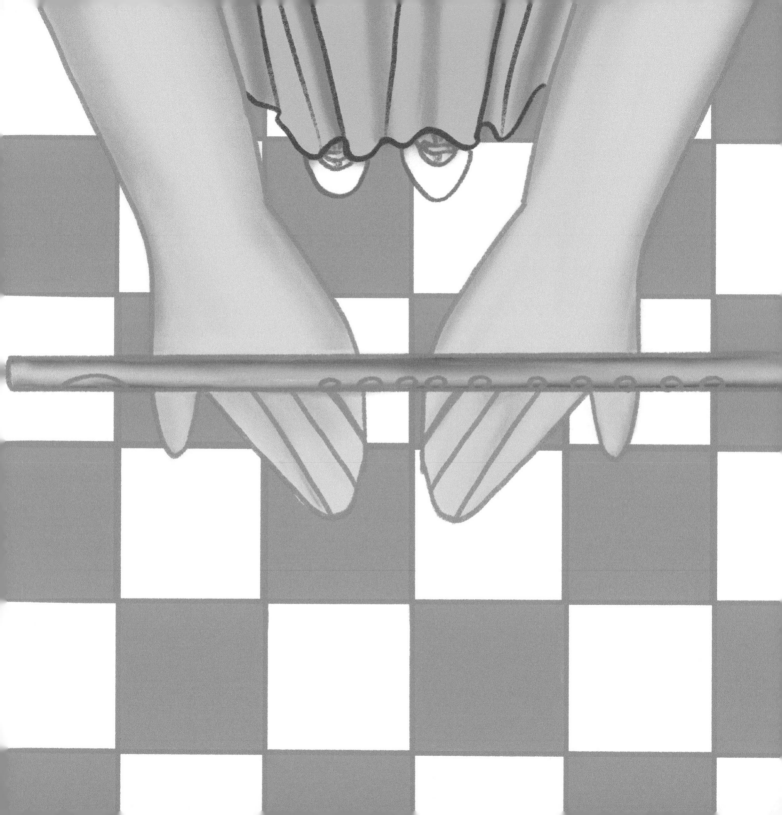

But the piccolo was just too small.

So she tried the tuba. It was large, and she felt so strong playing it, with its deep and low sound. It seemed like the tuba was exactly what she was looking for.

But the tuba was just too heavy.

So she tried the guitar. It wasn't too big,
it wasn't too small, and it wasn't too loud.
It seemed like the guitar was exactly
what she was looking for.

But the guitar had too many strings.

So she tried the triangle. It was easy to hold and easy to play, and Ruby loved the *ting, ting, ting* sound it made. It seemed like the triangle was exactly what she was looking for.

But the triangle was just too quiet.

Ruby felt defeated and decided she just couldn't find a way to be in her school's recital. She scratched her name off the signup list.

The next morning when Ruby arrived at school, her music teacher was waiting for her. She asked Ruby why she scratched her name off the signup list. Ruby told her that she just couldn't find an instrument. Her music teacher suggested the piano. She led Ruby to the music room, uncovered the piano, and adjusted the bench.

Ruby loved it! The piano made a beautiful sound. She wanted nothing more than to play the piano for the whole school. It wasn't too loud or too quiet. It was just right! It was exactly what she was looking for!

The big recital was finally here. Ruby had never been more proud. She had finally found her instrument.

Printed in the United States
By Bookmasters